OFF-ROADING VEHICLES

MILITARY VEHICLES

TAMRA B. ORR

Mitchell Lane
PUBLISHERS

Parent and Caregiver Tips for Creating Nonfiction Readers

The high-interest topics in the *Off-Roading Vehicles* series are sure to get your young reader excited about reading nonfiction. While exploring a fascinating subject, your reader will be introduced to new concepts, facts, ideas, and vocabulary.

Tips for Reading Nonfiction

Talk about Nonfiction

Explain that nonfiction books provide facts about real-world topics. When readers read nonfiction, they gain a rich understanding of the world. They build background knowledge that provides a foundation for learning and academic success.

Look at the Parts

This book contains the following helpful features. Share the purpose of each feature with your reader.

Photos, Captions, and Graphic Aids
The photos, captions, charts, maps, and other graphic aids in nonfiction texts contain a wealth of information. Help your reader identify different ways information can be displayed. A special feature, "A Closer Look," puts the spotlight on learning through images.

Sidebars
These extra tidbits of information help satisfy readers' curiosity and expand their knowledge.

Table of Contents
Located at the front of the book, this list shows the big ideas within the text and the page numbers where they can be found.

Glossary
Located at the back of the book, the glossary defines key words and phrases that are related to the topic. These words and phrases can be found in the text in **bold** type.

Comprehension Questions (Fact Check)
Multiple-choice questions help readers self-check to make sure they understand what they read.

Index
Located at the back of the book, the index is an alphabetical list of topics and the page numbers where they can be found.

With a little help and guidance, your reader will be on their way to enjoying and learning from nonfiction books.

Mitchell Lane
PUBLISHERS
mitchelllanepub.com

2001 SW 31st Avenue
Hallandale, FL 33009

First Edition, 2026.
Author: Tamra B. Orr
Designer: Kathy Walsh
Editor: Tricia Hoffman

Series: Off-Roading Vehicles
Title: Military Vehicles / by Tamra B. Orr

Hallandale, FL : Mitchell Lane Publishers, [2026]

Library bound ISBN: 979-8-89260-566-3
Paperback ISBN: 979-8-89260-597-7
eBook ISBN: 979-8-89260-570-0

Photo Credits
Adobe: background, miloje; Alamy: p21 & 29, dpa picture alliance; p8, mauritius images GmbH; p11, ZarkePix; p13, David Bokuchava; p20, GTCRFOTO; Kristoffer Tripplaar; Dreamstine: Cover & Title pg, Olegganki; p 19, Nfx702; p22, 23 & 29; Lance Cpl. Michelle Reig @wiki; Shutterstock: p14 & 28, LeStudio; p9 & 28, betto rodrigues; p10 & 28, Morphart Creation; p24 & 29, Oliver Hoffmann; p5, Michael Fitzsimmons; p6, Patrik Slezak; p7, Jonathan Weiss; p12, tomeqs; p13, Everyone-photo Studio; p16, The Image Engine; p17, Artistic Operations; p17, Boykov; p18, North Monaco; p26, Wirestock Creators; p27, mangostock

Contents

Tough Stuff

Armored bodies? √ Check.

Bulletproof windshields? √ Check.

A reliable vehicle that can protect its passengers and cover the toughest terrain?
√ Check and check.

Sounds like a military vehicle!

Some cars come with heated leather seats or expensive audio equipment. Others include solar-powered lights on the steering wheel. Some may have blind-spot and backup cameras.

And then, there are military vehicles.

Sure, they might have leather seats and special lights too. But they also have armored exteriors and bulletproof windshields! These tough vehicles are made to keep passengers protected every single mile.

FRONT

Not Just for the Military Anymore

Military vehicles were first created for the armed forces. They could move soldiers, carry equipment, and haul weaponry over all kinds of **terrain**.

These vehicles have armored bodies. They provide protection from bullets, bombs, and other threats. They're ready for **combat**.

But these vehicles are not just for the military anymore!

BUG OUT!

Most military vehicles are considered "bug out" vehicles, or BOVs for short. They are designed to get people to safety in emergencies like natural disasters.

Today, **civilians** are allowed to buy military vehicles. There are no federal laws against owning them. But some states do have rules about using them, because of their size, weight, and possible safety issues. Owners might need to get special permits or licenses.

Some military vehicles are used to protect **diplomats** during international travel. Others are used by celebrities or politicians. But thousands of these vehicles are used by families when they are off-roading.

A PRESIDENTIAL FLEET

Former U.S. president Barack Obama had 12 armored cars. They had thick, heavy doors and windows for protection. They came with fire alarm systems, night vision cameras, and even blood banks.

On the Battlefield

Military vehicles may look futuristic, but using them in battle is actually a very old idea. Even back in ancient Egypt, horse-drawn war **chariots** were used to carry soldiers and weapons.

The Army's first combat vehicles were used in 1916. Heavy trucks traveled 400 miles (643.7 km) over very rough terrain in the mountains of northern Mexico.

Soon after, thousands of these trucks were used in World War I. Many were used as ambulances, bringing wounded soldiers to medical care.

A Home with Civilians

By the late 1970s, civilians could buy military vehicles.

Some people wanted them for extra protection. But many people wanted them because they were different—and awesome!

Many were customized in special ways. Some owners added leather seats and sunroofs. Others installed night vision displays and **reinforced** bumpers.

Cadillac Escalade

Rolls-Royce Cullinan

COMPANY COMPETITION

Many car companies produce armored vehicles, including Chevrolet's Suburban and Tahoe, Toyota's Land Cruiser, Cadillac's Escalade, and even Rolls-Royce's Cullinan.

The Humvee

Few military vehicles are as recognizable as the Humvee. When it was first made, it was tested in all types of environments, from jungles to deserts. The Humvee could handle it all.

Thousands of Humvees were made for the U.S. Army, Marines, Air Force, and Navy. They carried everything from troops to missiles. They often worked as ambulances for the wounded.

Although the Humvee is only 6 feet (1.8 m) tall, it has a 16-inch (40.6-cm) **ground clearance**. It can roll over huge rocks, plow through deep water, tackle snow drifts, and clear the bumpiest trails.

In 1992, the Humvee became available to civilians. It was nicknamed the Hummer. Newer models have a lighter body and better gas mileage. Future models may be fully electric—and even driverless!

Police Interceptor

Police Interceptor SUV

THE INTERCEPTORS

Police officers across the country are coming to rely on Ford Police Interceptors®. Like military vehicles, Police Interceptors protect officers with fortified bodies to withstand collisions.

The G-Wagen

In the early 1970s, Mercedes-Benz® made the G-Wagen. G-Wagen is short for Geländewagen, which means cross-country vehicle in German. At first, they were made for the military. They were durable vehicles that could go almost anywhere.

By 1979, civilians could buy G-Wagens. But the design stayed the same.

In 1990, the G-Wagen became more **luxurious** for civilians. It was upgraded with special trim, leather seats, **cruise control**, anti-lock brakes, and **running boards**.

READY FOR SIX?

In 2013, a G-Wagen was made with six tires. It was popular in the Middle East. Its extra **traction** made it easier to climb tall sand dunes.

The G-Wagen is made for battle—but also for off-roading. It can drive over an 18-inch (45.7 cm) step, splash through three feet (0.9 m) of water, and climb steep hills.

G-Wagens are popular with celebrities. Actor and politician Arnold Schwarzenegger spent $1 million turning his G-Wagen into a fully electric model. Companies may begin doing the same in the future.

A RELIABLE RIDE

A man named Gunther Holtorf drove his G-Wagen to more than 200 countries and across 559,234 miles (900,000 km) over the course of 30 years. The vehicle did not break down once!

The Phantom Badger

The Phantom Badger was introduced by Boeing in 2013. The military uses it for medical **evacuation**, search and rescue, and more.

The Badger includes powerful **winches**, machine gun **turrets**, and grenade launchers. These military vehicles are small, only 5 feet (1.5 m) wide. They can fit inside an aircraft and be dropped directly into combat zones.

Boeing asked a team of NASCAR-experienced engineers to test the Phantom Badger. The team took the Badger off-roading in the desert.

The Badger has a suspension that can cover any terrain without making passengers bounce up and down. It can make a complete turn in tight spaces. Extra thick tires make it possible to roll over logs as big as telephone poles!

It's not currently available for civilians to buy, but it could be a possibility. "Boeing will gladly have a discussion with anyone interested in purchasing a Phantom Badger for their collection or personal use," says John Chicoli, Boeing's Phantom Badger program manager.

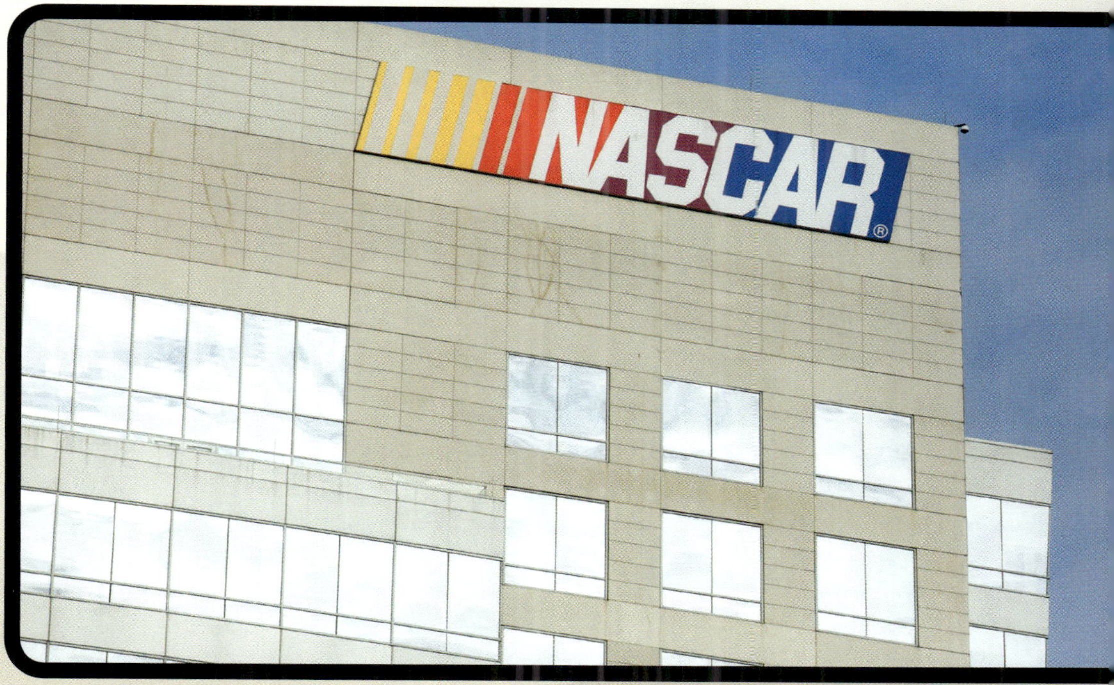
NASCAR

From the Battlefield to the Driveway

Military vehicles must be rugged and reliable. They must be able to handle all types of terrain, from thick, humid jungles to dry, windy sand dunes. They must be strong enough to carry troops and weapons on the battlefield.

But most importantly, they must keep everyone inside safe.

Luckily enough, many of these vehicles are also available for civilians to buy and enjoy. Time to head out and explore!

SIX-DIGIT PRICE TAGS

Military vehicles almost always come with hefty price tags, ranging from about $100,000 to $180,000 or even more.

A Closer Look

How do presidents travel with military vehicles internationally?

These military vehicles are loaded onto a special Air Force airplane and flown overseas, or wherever the president is visiting. They provide important and valuable protection for the president.

When were military vehicles used in ancient Egypt?

The horse-drawn chariot was introduced around 1600 BC. That's more than 3,600 years ago! Earlier chariots used oxen, but Egyptian chariots were usually pulled by horses and could travel faster.

How many Humvees does the U.S. military have?

More than 160,000! The military started using Humvees in the 1980s and still uses them today. Most Humvees can carry four to eight passengers.

Where did Gunther Holtorf travel in his G-Wagen?

Gunther, of Germany, traveled across six continents in his G-Wagen. Its name is Otto!

What are they doing with this Phantom Badger?

They're loading it onto a plane. The lightweight Phantom Badger is small enough to fit inside an aircraft, but it's still strong enough to cover the toughest terrain. It's also speedy—the Badger can reach speeds of up to 80 miles (128 km) per hour!

Where is this military vehicle?

It's driving across the Agafay Desert in Morocco, with the Atlas Mountains in the background. This desert is a stone desert, not sandy like the Sahara.

Glossary

chariots (CHAR-ee-uhtz)
a small vehicle pulled by a horse, used in battles in ancient times

civilians (suh-VIL-yuhnz)
those not in the armed forces

combat (KAHM-bat)
fighting between armies or people

cruise control (krooz kuhn-trohl)
a system that automatically maintains a vehicle's speed

diplomats (DIP-luh-mats)
people who officially represent their country's government in a foreign country as a job

evacuation (ih-vak-yoo-AY-shuhn)
the process of removing people from a dangerous place

ground clearance (ground KLEER-uhns)
the distance between the lowest part of a vehicle's undercarriage and the ground

luxurious (luhg-ZHOOR-ee-uhs)
being especially expensive or fine; nice to have but you do not really need

reinforced (ree-in-FORST)
strengthened with added support or material

running boards (RUHN-ning bordz)
boards extending along the side of a vehicle to help people get in and out

terrain (tuh-RAYN)
an area of land

traction (TRAK-shuhn)
the force that keeps a moving body from slipping on a surface

turrets (TUR-itz)
a structure that holds one or more guns

winches (WIN-chiz)
machines that lift or pull heavy objects

Fact Check

1. Some of the earliest military vehicles were _____.
   A. three-quarter ton trucks B. horse-drawn chariots C. ambulances
2. What is the Humvee's nickname?
   A. Hummer B. G-Wagen C. Hammer
3. What did Arnold Schwarzenegger spend $1 million doing?
   A. Buying a brand new Hummer B. Adding running boards to his Badger
   C. Turning his G-Wagen into an all-electric vehicle
4. Which military vehicle used NASCAR-experienced engineers to help with its design?
   A. Humvee B. G-Wagen C. Phantom Badger

Answers: 1. B, 2. A, 3. C, 4. C

Further Reading

DK. *Tank: The Definitive Visual History of Armored Vehicles.* DK Publishing, 2017.

Hansen, Grace. *Military Tracked Vehicles.* Abdo Publishing, 2016.

Hustad, Douglas. *US Army Equipment and Vehicles.* North Star Editions: Scholastic, 2021.

Pagel-Hogan, Elizabeth. *US Special Operations Forces Equipment and Vehicles.* North Star Editions, 2021.

On the Internet

Humvee Facts: 35 Things To Know About The HMMWV
militarymachine.com/humvee-facts/
Learn all about the Humvee and check out these 35 fascinating facts.

Military Vehicles
www.military.com/equipment/military-vehicles
Take a look at almost two dozen different types of military vehicles at Military.com.

Tank facts for kids
kids.kiddle.co/Tank
Explore cool facts about armored combat vehicles, specially geared toward kids.

Index

About the Author

Tamra B. Orr is a mom, wife, grandmother, and full-time writer and author living in the beautiful all-terrain Pacific Northwest. She lives in Oregon, home to the Oregon Military Museum that features tanks and other military vehicles. A graduate of Ball State University, Orr has written more than 750 nonfiction and educational books for readers of all ages and loves her job. It gives her the chance to learn about something new—and then share that information with readers of all ages—every single day.